I0436066

POLAR BEARS

Sandie Lee Books

Thanks for checking out the Sandie Lee Books Series. Please note: All Rights Reserved. No part of this publication may be reproduced in any form or by any means, including scanning, photocopying, or otherwise without prior written permission of the copyright holder. Copyright ©
2014

Polar Bears

There is only one species of the polar bear. In science, it is called, Ursus maritimus. This means "sea bear." The polar bear is the largest land predator and also the largest of all the bear species. The Inuit peoples have great respect for this bear. It is called, Nanuk. When they write about this animal they call it, Pihoqahiak. This means, the ever-wandering one. These fun facts are just the tip of the iceberg when it comes to the polar bear. Read on to discover more.

Where in the World?

Did you know the polar bear loves the ice and snow? This big burly bear lives mostly in the Arctic Circle, in the Arctic Ocean and all its areas. The polar bear loves the ice and the frigid waters of the Arctic and will spend a lot of its time in the water.

The Body of a Polar Bear

Did you know polar bears are huge? Male polar bears can weigh up to 1,700 pounds! Females are smaller at about 600 pounds, but still very big.   Adult males of this species can reach lengths of 10 feet long - that is as tall as a 1 story building!

Polar Bear Paws

Did you know the paws on this bear are suited to both water and snow? The polar bear's paws are huge - 12 inches across! On the bottom of the polar bear's big feet are pads covered with little bumps. These keep the bear from slipping on the ice and snow.

The Polar Bear's Fur

Did you know this bear's fur is waterproof? The polar bear's fur has 2 layers to it; a thick, short undercoat and longer top hairs. Even though the polar bear may appear to be white in color, the hairs on its coat are actually transparent (see through). Under the fur, this bear's skin is black to absorb the sunlight.

What a Polar Bear Eats

Did you know polar bears only eat meat? This type of animal is called, a carnivore. The main diet of the polar bear consists of the seal species. This bear has 42 teeth. They are very sharp and perfect for eating meat. The canine teeth (near the front) are longer and are used for grabbing and holding its prey.

The Polar Bear as a Predator

Did you know this bear is a still-hunter? The polar bear uses its excellent sense of smell to locate a seal. This is usually outside of a small hole in the ice the seal uses for getting air. When the seal comes up for a breath, the polar bear reaches in with its massive paw and drags it out.

The Polar Bear as Prey

Did you know the polar bear has no natural enemies, except man? The native people of the Arctic region hunted the polar bear for its hide and its meat. Every part of the bear was used. However, the native people only hunted the bear when it was needed. The polar bear is now protected from being poached.

The Polar Bear's Special

Did you know even though the polar bear is big, it is fast? This bear is an excellent swimmer. It spends a lot of time in the water. The polar bear can reach speeds of up to 6.2 miles-per-hour. The polar bear can also swim long distances - up to 62 miles without stopping.

Polar Bear Talk

Did you know this species of bear makes sounds? Adult polar bears mostly make sounds when they are unhappy. An angry polar bear may growl, hiss, chuff or champ its teeth together. Baby polar bears will whimper, squall, hiss and smack their lips. Mom polar bear will warn her cubs by chuffing or braying.

Polar Bear Mom

Did you know a female polar bear can have her young at 4 to 5 years of age? She will only breed about every 3 years. Mom polar bear will gain a lot of weight - over 400 extra pounds! She will build a den in the snow to have her young in.

Polar Bear Baby

Did you know baby polar bears are called, cubs? The cubs are born with soft fuzzy fur, they are blind and helpless. Usually, the female will have only 2 cubs, weighing around 2 pounds each. They nurse milk from their mother. Cubs will remain with mom for around 2.5 years.

Polar Bears at Rest

Did you know the polar bear likes to sleep on the ice and snow? This bear can rest in many positions. Sometimes it is sprawled out with all four legs spread. Other times, this bear may tuck its front legs under its chest. Often times it will sleep on its side.

Polar Bears at Play

Did you know this species of bear likes to play?
A polar bear will engage in play fighting. This
can be done by cubs, or by two young males
learning how to fight. Although, the polar bear is
mostly a solitary animal, it has been seen
embracing and playing with other bears for
hours on end.

Life of a Polar Bear

Did you know the polar bear usually lives to be 25 years-old? In the wild most polar bears rarely live past 25; however, one polar bear did live until she was 43 years-old. This bear was in captivity. Old or injured polar bears will usually die of starvation because they can no longer hunt for food.

Quiz

Question 1: What does *Ursus maritimus* mean?

Answer 1: Sea bear

Question 2: How big are the polar bear's paws?

Answer 2: Each one is 12 inches across

Question 3: What is the polar bear's favorite food?

Answer 3: Seals

Question 4: What does an angry polar bear do?

Answer 4: Hiss, chuff and champ its teeth together

Question 5: How old was the oldest polar bear?

Answer 5: 43 years-old

Thank you for checking out another addition from Sandie Lee Books! Make sure to check out Amazon.com for many other great titles.

www.ingramcontent.com/pod-product-compliance
Lightning Source LLC
Chambersburg PA
CBHW050925290526
45792CB00002B/883